3 4028 09284 1239
HARRIS COUNTY PUBLIC LIBRARY

J 599.767 Heo
Heos, Bridget
Do you really want to meet
a badger?

$8.99
ocn915774798

WITHDRAWN

W9-AOS-861

DO YOU REALLY WANT TO MEET A BADGER?

WRITTEN BY BRIDGET HEOS   ILLUSTRATED BY DANIELE FABBRI

Amicus Illustrated and Amicus Ink
are imprints of Amicus
P.O. Box 1329
Mankato, MN 56002

Copyright © 2017 Amicus. International copyright reserved in all countries. No part of this book may be reproduced in any form without written permission from the publisher.

Library of Congress Cataloging-in-Publication Data
Heos, Bridget, author.
Do you really want to meet a badger? / by Bridget Heos ; illustrated by Daniele Fabbri.
       pages cm. — (Do you really want to meet...wild animals?)
Audience: K to grade 3.
Summary: "A boy goes to a prairie to look for a badger in the wild and observes how they hunt"— Provided by publisher.
ISBN 978-1-60753-944-5 (library binding) –
ISBN 978-1-68152-115-2 (pbk.) —
ISBN 978-1-68151-062-0 (ebook)
1. Badgers–Behavior—Juvenile literature. 2. Badgers—Juvenile literature. I. Fabbri, Daniele, 1978- illustrator. II. Title.
QL737.C25H48 2016
599.76'7—dc23   2015029356

Editor: Rebecca Glaser
Designer : Kathleen Petelinsek

Printed in the United States of America at Corporate Graphics in North Mankato, Minnesota.

HC 10 9 8 7 6 5 4 3 2 1
PB 10 9 8 7 6 5 4 3 2 1

ABOUT THE AUTHOR

Bridget Heos lives in Kansas City with her husband, four children, and an extremely dangerous cat . . . to mice, anyway. She has written more than 80 books for children, including many about animals. Find out more about her at www.authorbridgetheos.com.

ABOUT THE ILLUSTRATOR

Daniele Fabbri was born in Ravenna, Italy, in 1978. He graduated from Istituto Europeo di Design in Milan, Italy, and started his career as a cartoon animator, storyboarder, and background designer for animated series. He has worked as a freelance illustrator since 2003, collaborating with international publishers and advertising agencies.

The badger is the mascot of your favorite team. But would you really want to meet one in the wild? You don't need to go far.

Badgers live throughout the West and Midwest in North America. Their habitats include deserts and prairies. A prairie has grass and wildflowers, and not many trees.

You're looking for a brown animal with a white stripe on its head and possibly its back. Its tracks are small. Look for five toes on each foot, with long claws on the front feet.

Badgers live underground. So look for
badger holes, too. Ouch! Found one.
Are you okay? Good.

If you could peer deep into the hole, you'd see the badger 10 feet (3 m) below, sleeping in its den. Badgers are nocturnal. They sleep during the day.

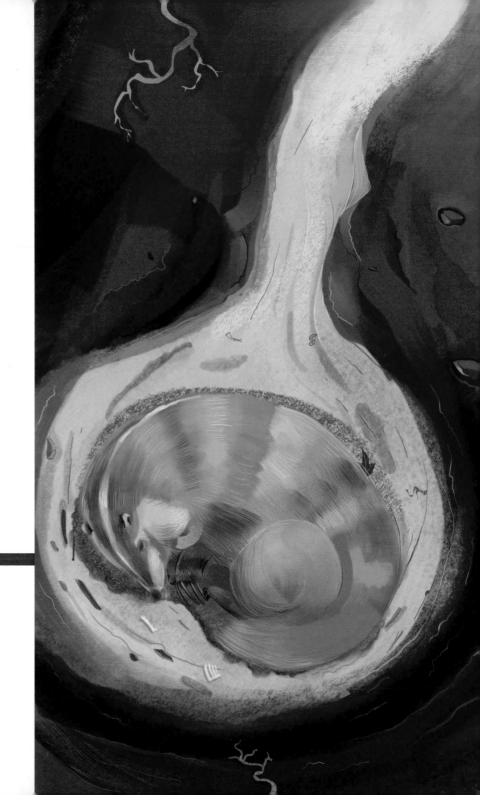

At dusk, the badger will come out to hunt. Badgers are carnivores. That means they eat other animals.

Here it comes! Grrrrrr. Uh-oh, looks like you're too close to its den. You'd better move back. Badgers growl and may even bite when they are threatened. They only weigh between 9 and 26 pounds (4–12 kg), but their bite is ferocious.

Yikes! Don't worry. The badger isn't jumping at you. It's going after that ground squirrel. Small rodents are a badger's favorite food.

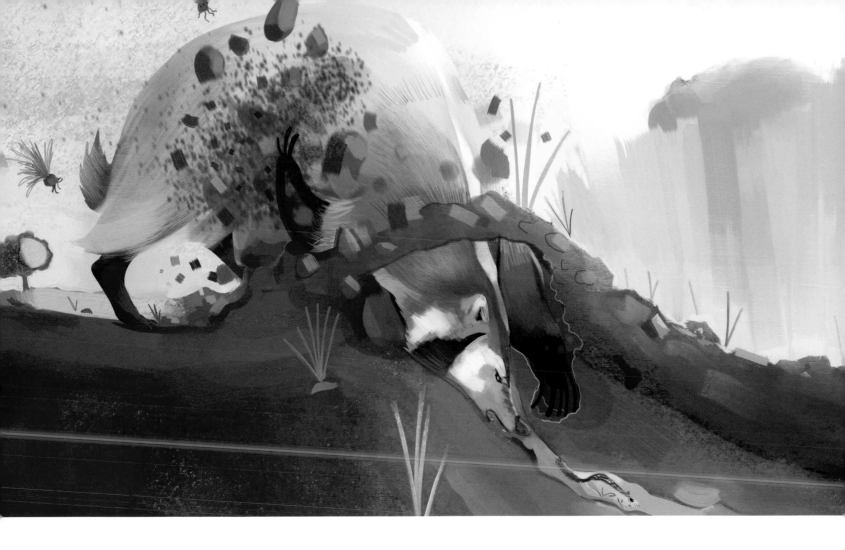

The ground squirrel jumps into a hole, and the badger chases it by digging. Its long, sharp claws make it an expert digger!

The badger can dig faster than the squirrel can run.

Yum! Fresh rodent.

Look, a coyote! It's hungry too.
Is it here to eat the badger?

No, it looks like the coyote wants to play. The coyote runs up to it. The badger jumps at the coyote, and the coyote trots away. The coyote is not just here for fun. Watch what happens.

The badger sniffs the ground. It smells a mouse.
Now, it digs. Oh, no! The mouse escaped
through another hole.

And now the coyote pounces on it! Like badgers, coyotes eat small animals. But coyotes can't dig as fast as badgers. So the coyote lets the badger do its dirty work!

Well, you haven't quite met a badger. And that's a good thing. If you'd gotten any closer, the badger may have bitten you! But you did get to see a badger in the wild. And it was awesome!

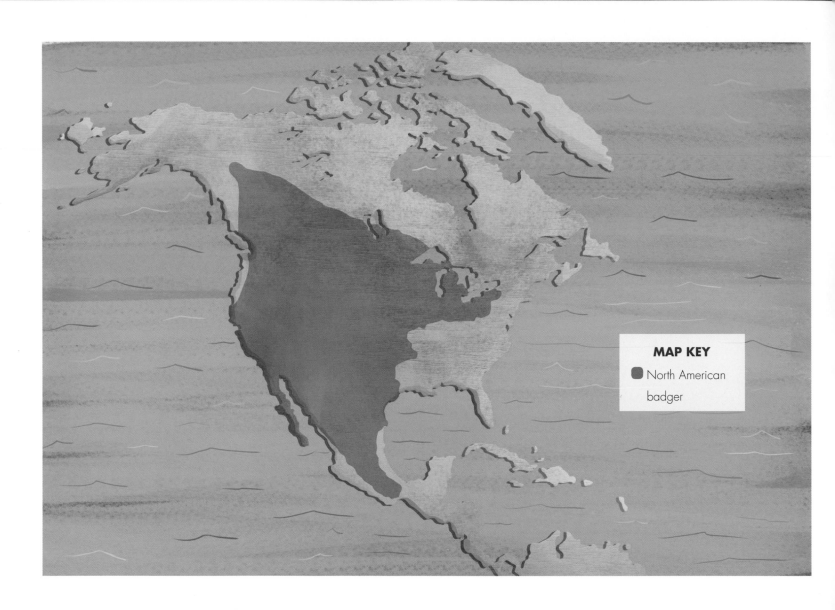

MAP KEY

● North American badger

GLOSSARY

carnivore An animal whose main diet is other animals.

den An animal's home in the wild; badger dens are holes dug in the ground or in hillsides.

dusk The time of day when it begins to get dark.

habitat An animal's natural environment.

nocturnal Being active mainly at night.

prairie A large area of flat or rolling grassland with few trees.

rodent A mammal with large front teeth that keep growing, such as rats, mice, and squirrels.

Harris County Public Library
Houston, Texas

READ MORE

Llanas, Sheila Griffin. Coyotes.
Minneapolis: ABDO, 2013.

Maximus, Sofia. **Badgers in the
Dark**. New York: Gareth Stevens,
2013.

Phillips, Dee. **Badger's Burrow**. New
York: Bearport Publishing, 2013.

Zobel, Derek. Badgers.
Minneapolis: Bellwether Media,
2012.

WEBSITES

**BIOKids: Kids' Inquiry of Diverse Species:
American Badger**
www.biokids.umich.edu/critters/Taxidea_taxus/
Read about the habitat, behavior, and life cycle of the
American badger.

Environmental Education for Kids:
Do You Want to Be a Badger?
dnr.wi.gov/eek/critter/mammal/badger.htm
Learn why the badger is the state animal of Wisconsin.

National Park Service:
Bandelier National Monument: American Badger
www.nps.gov/band/learn/nature/badger.htm
View a badger photo gallery and read about the badgers
that live in this national park in New Mexico.

Wildscreen Archive: American Badger
*www.arkive.org/american-badger/taxidea-taxus/
video-11a.html*
Watch a video of a badger and coyote hunting in the wild,
plus view badger photos.

*Every effort has been made to ensure that these websites are appropriate for
children. However, because of the nature of the Internet, it is impossible to
guarantee that these sites will remain active indefinitely or that their contents
will not be altered.*